# CONTINUING TO . . . .
# MAKE MATTERS VERSE

## Les D. Pearce

ARTHUR H. STOCKWELL LTD
Torrs Park, Ilfracombe, Devon, EX34 8BA
*Established 1898*
*www.ahstockwell.co.uk*

By the same author:
*Making Matters Verse*
*The Love Verses*

ISBN 978-0-7223-4637-2
*Printed in Great Britain by*
*Arthur H. Stockwell Ltd*
*Torrs Park    Ilfracombe*
*Devon  EX34 8BA*

For Anne,
who brings to life my scribblings.

# PROFILE

I'm a pub dweller; I love my beer and the atmosphere of the pub. I have always got inspiration for my writing from the characters therein – pub poetry. It eases me away from some of the deep stuff. I try to keep a balance! Alcohol has always been a big part of my life . . . a confidence booster; I was very shy.

Older now, wiser? Who knows? I am intrigued by words and by trying to recreate the structure of traditional verse. I don't know whether I succeed, but for as long as I may I will keep trying.

# AUDACIOUS PRETENDER

Audacious pretender! Too late for me?
(The style is old; it doesn't 'rock and roll')
To mould and shape the lines in symmetry
With splendid words plucked from the very soul.

Born out of time? I may have had a chance!
When wordsmiths plied their trade with skills supreme.
A shaky-speare! Perhaps a trembly lance!
My nervous pen would match them in a dream.

Still I attempt to hold the specialness
These precious pearls long sunk in waters deep
To salvage treasures from the wordy mess
Pretender me! Am I the one to keep

The beauty of the rhythm and the rhyme?
What chance success . . . for one born out of time?

# FOREWORD

As my reader will already be aware, this anthology is the sequel to *Making Matters Verse*, a resounding failure, to date, in the literary field and bestseller lists.

The thought springs to mind: if there is nobody reading this stuff, why bother to write it, let alone publish?

It can only be the heady mixture of ego-insanity.

May I acknowledge the publishers (few writers do!) and all the hard work they put into the finished product. They take us on – in the nicest possible way.

# FANTASY – YOU WAIT! YOU SEE!

You wait!
I'll catch the sea and sky;
My words will damp a dreamer's eye!

You see!
My verse will come to bloom;
And lighten all the dark and gloom!

For I am gifted;
I have all the magic that I need
And when I'm lifted
Those who seek a specialness will read . . .

. . . Of love and colours; flowers;
Skies alive with shifting clouds;
Of scents from summer showers;
And of solitude; and crowds . . .
Of angels; I will move the souls of mortals, watch me fly!

You wait! You see!
You follow me!
For I am reaching high!

Here's poetry and more; a soul exposed;
Here's nakedness; revealings. Furthermore . . .
I've boldly gone – although I've gone before.
Here's deeper stuff; more private thoughts disclosed.
For poets keep their minds just slightly closed
And should you gently ease the half-closed door . . .
Here's poetry, and more!

Here's poetry and more. I'm well disposed
I've searched my inner limits to explore
The sonnet; rhythmic rondeau; verse galore!
There's drama; humour; tragedy enclosed.
Here's poetry, and more.

# CONTENTS

## Darkness, Dreams and Erotica

## Social Comment

## Family Matters

## Reflections on Perfection

## Illumination

## Love

## Potpourri

# DARKNESS, DREAMS AND EROTICA

Come the dark night's deathly trance
When freedom lets the spirit dance . . .
*'The Spirit Dance'*

# SENSATION

Oh stimulation
Masturbation
Searching for
The sweet sensation
Fascination
King's Cross Station
Therein lurks
Crude copulation
Oh such frustration
No elation
Day has gone
No titillation
Saturation
Perspiration
Wherein lies
The sweet salvation
Sweet expiration
Transportation
Spirit come
In exultation
Explanation
Jubilation
Praise to God
For His Creation.

# DEATH AND DREAMS

And now he comes in dreams – a wanderer;
A living corpse demanding more of me.
I'm frightened! Shocked awake! A ponderer
Half dreaming still – are dreams reality?
He comes in dreams and beggars sanity.

He cannot be! Yet, here he is for real.
He haunts my sleep; he stands pathetically! . . .
And now I'm left with guilt. An overspill
Of what I should have done, then do I feel?
What feeling when I left in time of need?

He's gone to dust, but here he is for real!
And dreams become reality indeed.

A wanderer, he staggers through my dreams
Reality may not be what it seems.

# POETRY! TRY POE

Not bedtime reading when the lights are low
Black ravens in mid-nightmare hover there
But, if you want 'dark poetry' try Poe

And if you've read of Usher's fall you'll know
Of vaulted catacombs and . . . Hark! I swear
I heard a screaming way down there below

No brightness in a mind so dense – oh no!
I could not hearten you, I would not dare
But should you want 'dark poetry' try Poe

Who else would tell of dead hearts beating slow?
And who could catch the horror with *his* flair?
He's scared me half to death I'll have you know!

Here's wan, frail maidens, pure as driven snow
Who rise like wraiths from coffins – be aware
That if you crave 'dark poetry' try Poe

'Is all we see or seem [Here's Poe in flow] . . .
A dream within a dream?' (A mystic air)
Such words can leave a chill in afterglow
So, if you want 'dark poetry' try Poe.

# THE SKELLINGTONS (*sic*) OF HELL

The gates of hell are lined by grinning skellingtons
Grey naked bones, unclothed – except for wellingtons
Black rubb'ry lumps on spindly bony legs –
Sad skellingtons – they step amongst the dregs
They slip and slide on hellish gore and slime
In life they had a really wondrous time

They stepped on all – gave nought for treading soft
And heeded not the good way – they just scoffed!
The best was theirs: rude health, good clothes, nice shoes,
Real comfort drugs, and sex, and loads of booze!!
They may have raped and murdered – who can know?
Now in the afterlife they're down real low

The skellingtons of hell have earned their place
Dear Lucifer has granted them his grace
He's give 'em boots – protection for their feet
A 'carer' he can be so very sweet
He will not let them soil their bony toes
Here's hell enough! It's gruesome – heaven knows!

In conversation skellingtons remark
Of past deeds that they've done – they have a lark
Their reminiscences would make you squirm
But now they're low, much lower than a worm!
So, man and demon always in cahoots
Forsaken souls for just a pair of boots.

# SLEEPING PARTNER

The darkness always frightened him!
Sometimes in the deathly quiet of night
It seemed the whole world had died
And he was alone. Alone except for the ghosts.
Always the ghosts. He couldn't actually see or hear them
But he knew they were there.

When he had to go to the bathroom
In the middle of the night;
This was a worrying time! After he'd peed
And turned the light off he sensed
He was being watched;
Could he get back to the safety of his bed
Before he was grabbed by somebody; some thing?

What a fool this boy is! He thinks that he's safe
After closing the bedroom door.
Doesn't he realise that they (the ghosts)
Walk straight through solid objects?
Doesn't he realise they can walk straight through him,
Or just stand in him?

Perhaps, all his life a ghost has stood inside him;
Possessed him; animated him. And when he sleeps
And the ghost decides to wander
Freely for a while, to lurk in dark corners
With its own kind . . . suddenly
It is blinded by a bathroom light –
And it waits for the right moment!

# THE POET'S NIGHTMARE

The night was silent, now the moon had gone
And blackness, as if from the depths of hell,
Ascended through the room where light had shone
And all abroad there seemed an evil spell . . .
Was cast; and omens did not augur well.

The poet, heavy-eyed, just could not keep . . .
Awake. Then, in his dream, a phantom bell
Resounded till he started up from sleep.

With eyes wide staring into darkness deep:
"Beelzebub! You found my sacred place!"
Then, through a crack, a phosphorescent seep
Took on the Devil's form with leering face

And thus intoned, with rasping, fetid breath:
"Your sonnets stink and **you** are done to death!"

# THANK GOD FOR BRIGHTNESS IN THE MORNING SKY

And I have slept too long!

A while ago in heavy sleep
I wandered, lost,
Along the creepy tunnels, shadowed, deep
In dreams I tossed
Where demons lurk, and gasp their hellish breath
Upon my face
Just out of reach from claws, from dreaded death.
Escape! There! A glow, a safer place.
Wake now! Too long has stayed the night
And dark holds fear!
My cowering spirit yearns for daylight, bright,
Unshadowed, clear.
Through double glaze and heavy-lidded eye
The view astounds!
Deep pink and purple streaks, the morning sky
Seems painted. White seagulls shriek their sounds!

And yet the dark *was* there?

But see the glow! This hallowed dawn,
God's heaven shines
Through windows with their pastel curtains drawn
And all the signs
Of miracles and joy are on display
For all to see
And beauty beams across the breaking day.
Lord, light up my way, unburden me

For I have slept too long!

God creates the magic words
In heaven, so below it
Some mortal with the soul inspired
May call himself a poet.

Twilight gloom
Drink besotted.
All is doom!
Nothing jotted . . . but wait; some inspiration . . .

## THE DEVIL OF A CONSCIENCE

The Devil has me in his sight
He tempts with evil thought
Of lusty things that will delight
"Come, come, your soul is bought."

Then conscience (with its air of grace;
Its 'holier than thou')
Bids "Heed him not, avert your face."
I'm trying hard, but how?

At certain times the instincts crave
Forbidden naughty fruits.
It's then old Lucifer (the knave)
And I are in cahoots.

When nubile nymphs invade my dreams
And force me to submit
To all their carnal lurid schemes
I want no part of it!

As demons hold me fast asleep
And tempt with sins sublime
Old conscience grasps me from the deep
And wakes me just in time!

I lie there in the dark, bemused.
'Seemed all was going well'
Enjoying being used, abused
How heaven-like this hell.

But therein lies the Devil's guile
He strikes a saintly pose.
The giveaway? The leering smile
And hooves instead of toes.

So get behind you, tempters all,
You godforsaken band.
I'm reaching upwards from the Fall
To grasp our Saviour's hand.

# ERATO

When once all was a wonderland;
Where stars shone on a silver sea;
Where golden moonlight clothed the sand;
And all was hushed serenity.

A sculptured goddess bathed in light,
Whose dark eyes held all mystery,
Emerged into this magic night
Her form was fashioned perfectly.

She danced upon the moonlit sand
A naked ballet; perfect grace.
No man could ever touch her hand,
Nor breathe a kiss upon her face.

Light-fingered shadows stroked her form;
A crystal in her navel shone.
In man she could create a storm
She; mortals dare not look upon!

A son of Neptune stood close by
The guardian of this special one.
She was the sea; she was the sky,
Desired e'er since time begun.

In silence she performed her dance.
Unwatched she moved, cavorted free.
But fate and dreams allowed, perchance
That I was privileged to see.

She'd bend and stretch, then turn and squirm
A moment, arched, and then a thrust.
Her shining body bronzed and firm
Yet I could only stare nonplussed.
(Away all thoughts of dev'lish lust) . . .

. . . Just then the dream began to die
This beauty turned her back to me
Mosaic crystal sparked my eye
Then she was gone beneath the sea.

Could I have really stood alone?
Beheld a heav'nly dance displayed?
Then, on the sand, the magic stone!
That in her navel cup had laid.

And sometimes on a moon-bright night
When stars shine on a silver sea,
A crystal gaze shall bring delight –
Erato! Dance your dance for me.

# COMINGS AND GOINGS

She took my hand and led me through the trees
We found a quiet place, like paradise
The sun was warm, there was a gentle breeze
And she was soft and oh so very nice.

I'd seen her in a dream a while ago
I caught her smile through misty haze of sleep
She was a nymph; a naughty so-and-so
Who gave this beau much more than just a peep!

If dreams may be a hint of what's to come
And there are maidens firm! And ripe! And keen!
Of upturned breast and perfect rounded bum
Then, may I go where once I'm sure I've been?

A pleasing little interlude was spent
She beckoned, come, and when I came . . . she went.

# SELF-ABUSE

Forty press-ups; off I go

I've done this thing for years
I'm fifty-plus and getting slow
Yet still I grunt and still I blow
And take the pain
Of muscle strain
And sweat away the beers.

The hurdle stretch; self-torture

But great for spine and thighs!
It says so on the mat I use
An exercise in self-abuse
Yet when I pose
The ego grows
The mirror never lies!!

I'm sexually attractive?

The torso toned and firm.
But who on earth will you impress
With all this postured nakedness
Exhale and see
The gut hang free
Enough to make one squirm.

Yet still I hang on in there

And force the heart to pump
And circulate the blood around
This fitness freak must stand his ground
But when to stop?
Or just to drop!
A muscled . . . lifeless . . . lump.

# NARCISSISTIC

From this angle looking down my eyes have caught
The curves and lines.
Sculptured breasts are firm; the belly flat and taut
Not yet the signs . . .

. . . Of age! Sleek, with muscle still, not gone to flab!
Not yielded yet
To great amounts of McDonalds and kebab!
Look further! Get . . .

. . . A voyeur's-eye view of legs: long, strong and sprawled.
Vain one, it's you!
Statuesque Greek god! By what name are you called?
**NARCISSUS** who?

# SENSUALITY IN OLD AGE

It's hard to keep one's body firm – it's hard
Maintaining a desirable physique!
Oh love me, my beloved! Don't discard . . .
A willing spirit, less than once a week!

Can we love as young ones love? No, never!
For we have reached the age where flesh is weak.
Can we make such music, sweet, together?
Or shall we end up lying cheek to cheek?

A warrior am I with armour bright,
Impassioned by the battle. I have come
To lay beside my maiden of the night
And to her soft caress I shall succumb.

In truth the ageing process makes one wilt.
The lance can only manage half a tilt.

# HEARTBURN; PANIC

Surging pains within the chest
The grim policeman lingers
To make a cardiac arrest!
But what of tingling fingers? . . .

. . . And pain that travels through the arm?
All seems to be all right.
Yet wakened by the fire alarm
The heart's been set alight!

Fast-forward ten days; still the pain
Severe distress I feel.
The doctor listens, notes the strain
Prescribes a barium meal.

"The heart is strong I know the signs
The symptoms would suggest
The stomach or the intestines
We'll do this X-ray test."

Fast-forward four weeks; great relief
No cancers beyond cure.
No lurking ulcers causing grief
These tubes of mine are pure!

At last the pain subsides and so
It seems old doc was right.
When heartburn sets the chest aglow
Don't panic in the night.

# LOOSE CONNECTIONS

Dare I hope there's other things? . . .
I dreamed I flew with angel's wings
How real it was! I floated high
Beyond the earth; beyond the sky;
Just pushed, then with a natural ease
I drifted up above the trees.
Then upward further, gaining height,
A strange somnambulistic flight.
And though I dreamed, it seemed that I
Was wide awake! And I could fly!
My senses all were clear and sharp
I heard no sweet celestial harp
Nor saw no demons out in space . . .
Just floated with an eagle's grace.

I'm sure there must be other things
Such realism dreaming brings.
At night I bid the world goodbye
Deep sleep; then moribund I lie
With just a hint of shallow breath
Alive – yet very close to death.
This earthbound thing is padded stuff.
I hold that dreams are true enough.
A fleeting glimpse of what is real.
A body light; ethereal
Equipped for what is meant to be.
Unburdened for eternity.
So let me fly when sleep is nigh
Beyond the earth; beyond the sky.

# SOCIAL COMMENT

Preposterous verses!
To hell with the curses!
*'The Spirit Dance'*

# A VEGETARIAN'S NIGHTMARE
(Suddenly Everyone Thinks They're a Poet!)

Great chunks of steak (not too well done,
A carrot on the side)
Cooked tender so the blood may run
"Such succulence!" he cried

God save me from the fools; enough!
Go crunch on celery
Just serve me meat and sim'lar stuff
And happy I shall be

Lord, give me ham and beef and lamb
(The coleslaw if you must)
And tinned corned beef – old-fashioned Spam
And meat pie with a crust

And sausages done to a turn
Sunk deep in Yorkshire pud
Crisp onions with a hint of burn
The taste is awful good

My wat'ring mouth – be still! Be still!
Fried fish in battered crumb
God's creatures ready for the kill
There's plenty more to come.

# SHAGGED

They've got two dogs.
Her: the remote look of a wife
Who's been shagged by her spouse
As a routine; and done
Without pleasure.

As dead as logs
But still, her dogs are full of life –
She's eyes just like a mouse . . .
Afraid. But dogs are fun.
Some brief leisure.

She's blank; spaced out!
Appearance? Well, she's dressed quite nice
Yet hardly says a word
"A double vodka, ice"
Then one cold stare.

She'd scream (no doubt)
"Hush" dogs know well of men and mice;
Relationships absurd.
Their frisky needs suffice
Small comfort there.

Shagged by her life!
Existence! Is it worth the time?
She's vulnerable and lost
But not these poxy dogs.
Their lives are charmed.

"Here's me; this wife;
No kids, just dogs! A bleedin' crime.
Whose fault? It's mine. What cost?"
Two people dead as logs . . .
Alive embalmed.

# THREE CHEERS

. . . And suddenly we've done two thousand years.
I hear there's celebrations all about.
Two thousand years. Three cheers! Let's hope he hears.
Hip hip hooray! His brethren scream and shout.

Let's hope he hears; let's pray he takes the time. . . .
Two thousand years – we haven't learned a lot.
Perfected things: pollution, war and crime.
So, what we've sown is what we now have got.

I hear there's celebrations; fun galore
Another barbecue; a bonfire night?
Let's light the skies with bright but let's ignore
The sorriness of man's pathetic plight.

Hip hip hooray! We've done two thousand years.

Then Jesus wept and clouds rained down God's tears.

# ALONE

Into the pool a pebble's thrown
And in the end you stand alone.
To be a wealthy rolling stone
Or king, supreme, upon his throne
Still – in the end you stand alone.

Soon science will create a clone
"It can't be right," we'll have a moan
God save us all from Adam's bone
And in the end you're on your own.

There's modem tech – the mobile phone,
Computers – till the fuse is blown
The mugger's victim may well groan
There's no one there! You're on your own.

So on your own you struggle through
A family, kids, divorce, what's new?
This cauldron pot of human stew
Are we for real? The chosen few?

You stand alone, believe! It's true.
There's only God and time and you
There is no ship, no hearty crew
Delivering the special brew
It's up to you! I'm sure you knew!

Thank God for death and colds and flu
And all Creation two by two
But why the saving? Where's the clue?
A place for us in life's *Who's Who?*
Into the pool a pebble's thrown
But in the end we stand alone.

# IT'S DIFFICULT FOR DENNIS

Dennis lost his mate a while ago
Since then he seems remote
Oh sure! He wears the mask, but still we know
The telltale lump that hits his throat . . .

. . . In conversation of old Tom.

Dennis moved – not far – just up the road
But when you're getting on
Uprooting; changing – such a heavy load.
Soon Christmas and his mate is gone

That's when he went and died – old Tom.

Difficult for Dennis Tom's not here
They were real close; good pals.
Their days were full of laughs and drinking beer
Then life just ends and gloom prevails . . .

But bright and cheery was old Tom.

It's difficult for Dennis.

# TELEGRAPHIC WIT
### (*Daily Telegraph,* 23 January 2001)

He had a wit – like none before
'Passed over' gone 'beyond the door'
A mortal man – he's nothing more –
A genius? To some a bore!
He raised a smile; stuck in the craw
Spoke truths of politics and law
Attacked his prey with tooth and claw
Extolled the rich, decried the poor
Free verse he hated – that's for sure
So here's my rhyme for Auberon Waugh.

# PHILOSOPHY OF AN IDIOT

Who said,
'Each day is joyful – just begun'?
Some plonker
With a queer idea of fun!

We're all aware of trauma
Come the dawn
The stagg'ring off to work
In early morn.

Who said,
'You'll reap the benefit of work
No worries in retirement'?
What a burk!

We're slaughtered at the start
And at the end
Whoever said it's great
Is round the bend.

# DISTURBANCE

I hear its cry; sporadic monotone
It grates my nerves
Incessant; "For Christ's sake, I'm trying
To concentrate."

Can a child's wailing be more important
Than poetry?

You are born and noisy
My silent words await their birth.

Quiet now! You must have captured my thought
Sleep, child. Please, stay slept
Give my thoughts a chance to scream:
I hear its cry. . . .

# THE IMPORTANCE OF DISCIPLINE

Revere the child and cosset him
As if he were a god.
Absorb the shocks with well-placed cotton wool
Then out he steps one ignorant
Obnoxious little sod
Who thinks he's great, but God knows he's a fool.

Mostly all the kids are rough
Without a sense of guilt.
The teachers say they do the best they can
And parents all are weak enough
Yet proud of what they've built!
Moronic child becomes moronic man.

# DOING GOOD

He sauntered down his merry path
He mugged old ladies "What a laugh."
He sniffed the glue; he took the drugs
He wasn't like the other thugs!
He had a brain! But he had been abused
And counselling had left him more confused.

He'd never even thought he may be bad!
Okay, he'd go for 'dodgy' never 'mad'
He'd just do unto others what they did
(The adults would neglect the little kid)
And deep down in his mind he saw a way
"You took from me and each dog has its day."

They filled his mind with loads of crap
Clear consciences were all on tap
"It wasn't you who did the deed
But others sowed an evil seed
Just carry on, be sure you have no guilt"
And what a monster do-gooders have built!

# HOUSEBREAKING (1996)
(As We Forgive Those Who Trespass Against Us!!)

Someone broke into our flat, removed the louvred glass
Squeezed through the space
Went through the place
(We'd gone away) – and so it came to pass . . .

. . . Stole little bits and pieces, turned the bedroom upside
down
No damage done?
What joy! What fun!
Who winds it up? What animates the clown?

Constabulary on the scene; responding took a time.
No great relief!!
No captured thief!!
"Secure the place" . . . Cost? . . . Ninety quid; a crime!

I s'pose the law has lots to do and we are just small fry
But facts are facts
We pay the tax
And confidence is gone when they don't try.

So here we are back from our hols and listing stolen goods
Our agent came
Insurance claim
'A portable typewriter' Mrs Woods.

On the whole it's not too bad. It could have been much worse
Remain brave-faced
Goods soon replaced
But until then I have to *write* the verse.

Someone out there knows our home. Some stranger came within
It came and left
For petty theft
No grievous harm, thank God, no mortal sin.

And there's the *Life of Jesus* conspicuous by its size
Maybe the crook
Did spy the book!
And sensed the Lord with penetrating eyes.

'Thou shalt not steal.'

# ZERO TOLERANCE

The yob will only put up with so much before he turns ugly.
   He didn't mean no harm? He rode his bike where he let his
dog crap and where he gobbed; on the pavement!
   The Sid Vicious school of elegance and charm had taught
him well!
   Then a policeman stopped him! The shock was too much;
he was offended; the policeman apologised?


Let's 'ave some zero tolerance round 'ere.
Let's see some coppers' presence on the street.
Cos sure as hell nice people walk in fear
For yob and slob they're guaranteed to meet.

There's dogs' crap and there's bikers on the path
All criminal offences – so we're told.
Yet law enforcement! What a bloody laugh!
God help the frail, the vulnerable, the old!

"Graffiti! Man, it's inner-city art!
The kids are bored; they like to spray the walls!
They like to swear! They like to belch and fart!
What law and order? What a load of balls!"

Athletic muggers jump their prey and run.
Then some old girl lies bleeding, shocked and bruised.
Oh! what a laugh; oh! what a bit of fun!
Take note, you b------s, we are not amused!

44

Come back, you copper; you who got respect!
Who wouldn't stand no nonsense from the youth.
Instilling what was **morally** correct
Not taking any mouth from the uncouth.

Come back and reprimand the naughty ones
And capture them before it is too late.
Before the water pistols turn to guns
Before the country's in a sorry state.

Perhaps too late! Low profiles stayed **too** low?
Free rein was given, far too much, too long.
Moronic, embryonic, urged to grow!
The meek inherit fear . . . and it's all wrong.

Hey! . . . 'zero tol-er-ance' . . . a catchy phrase.
It's got street cred, it slips cool off the tongue.
It's nothing new! We had it in the days
When streets weren't out of bounds . . . when I was young.

Let's 'ave some zero tolerance round 'ere
Cos sure as hell **nice** people walk in fear.

# THE BUSINESS OF MERCY

The insult of the do-gooder:
"If you were there to watch them die
You would be grieved as much as I."

Response from realist:
"Dare you insult the ones who know
The ones whose pain will ever grow?
And if you watched as it did gloat
While slitting some poor bastard's throat
And if you saw it walk away –
And smiling as its victim lay
And if this one it killed was yours
Then maybe we would hear applause
As in death's chair you saw it placed
Shocked! Terrified! and ashen-faced.

"Deterrent this is not," I hear!
Yet lastly it must taste the fear
It goes some way to ease the pain
And never shall it kill again.

The business of mercy is God's.

# FAMILY MATTERS

A fraying cord that time has worn
The line will end; no child will mourn . . .
*'An Older Sister'*

# 12 BLONDIN STREET

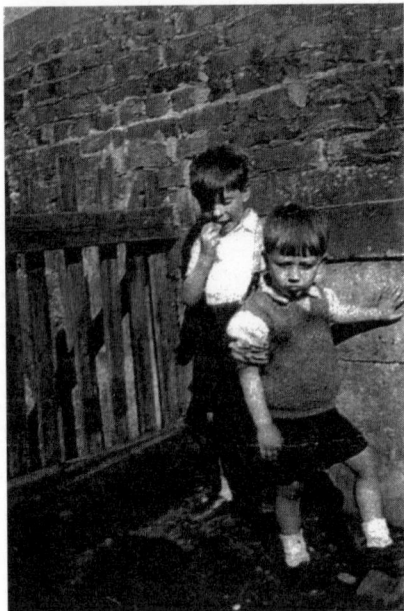

**BOW, LONDON E3**

# BACKYARD

Hey, kids! Just smile! Say cheese!
Quick! Click – two lads in freeze
With scruffy knees.

In camera posed – then caught
Slum kids – the surly sort –
But deep in thought . . .
It's our backyard, our place
For now it's all the space
A kid can face.

And catch the one behind
Developing his mind
The pensive kind.
The minder stands his ground
'My mate' he's been around
Aggressive hound.

# SCULLERY

The steam, the rattling saucepan lids
The butler sink
And there was Mum "I loved my kids"
It makes you think
Was this the start of something wrong?
A stifled scream!
Some slight control, but swept along
A steady stream!
There always was some Flo or Lil
To chat a while
And Mum amid the steam, she still found
Time to smile.
I reckon she had real despair
Now I reflect
A bold attempt at love and care
No disrespect.

Depressed. I turned the gas up high
I had these spots
Dramatic suicide! I'd die
Among the pots
No pain, deep breaths, quick as a blink
I'd slip away
Such drama at our kitchen sink
But not today.

# AND THE REST

A front room, back room,
Two bedrooms and *stairs*
Real basics here, old Dad he squandered dough
It wasn't much
It wasn't even theirs
They let it go in Blondin Street in Bow

A marriage gone to pot – a sad affair
Our mum confused. She got this other bloke
And Father said he didn't really care
A sorry tale or just a bloody joke?
Dad stayed at home
They went their separate ways
Mum said she couldn't leave
For 'our kids' sake'
A wrong decision
Dark became the days
Indifference, till Father made the break

So ends the first instalment – woe, oh woe!
It all went wrong in Blondin Street in Bow.

# NO COMMON GROUND
(Final Instalment)

No common ground
So what of blood ties now?
No doubt it was just sham, pretend
Who said we should be close?
Who showed us how?
Be sure you made it clear to end.

No common ground
There never was, just cold
A no-man's bleak and freezing land
I have it now
And should I get too old
I'll take no comfort from your hand.

# CHRISTMAS JOY
## (God Bless Joan Elsie)

What fun Mum had at Christmas time – what joy!
Each moment packed with seasonal 'delight'
Her bright-eyed kids who would not sleep *this night*
And one drunk husband she could not employ.

Such endless fun! And nothing could destroy
Our mum's intent to make it all *go right*
Leftovers greasy – *not a pretty sight*
But she had full-cream sherry – *boy, oh boy*

She must have had *some* fun, she seemed *quite* calm
She pulled a cracker, wore a paper hat
And had her photo took linked arm in arm . . .
With Dad? We never thought she'd come to that.

But then, the full rich glass Mum never missed
Survival of the fittest . . . or the pissed.

# PORTRAIT OF A CHARACTER

When his dad was blown to bits
The whisky got him through the Blitz
It eased the fear and stopped the s---s (bowel movements).

And in his life of hit and miss
Our dad has ever sworn by this
Not one for beer it makes him p--s (urinate).

Of government and upper class;
"All traitors" as he drains the glass,
"They all need kicking up the a--e"(buttocks).

"Corruption in the power halls;
Encouragement of criminals;
What justice? What a load of balls"
(a shortened version of the offensive word b------s).

With immigration far too great
An overburdened welfare state
"The masses sure can copulate" (this replaces the F-word).

Young women in the tabloids – nude
And flaunting homosexuals – crude
No decency – just bloody rude.

He's nearing eighty – been about
Somewhat deaf and tends to shout
But only swears when it slips out – metaphorically speaking.

And as it happens, by and by,
He got quite ill but didn't die
All down to **Anno Domini** . . .

. . . His doctor said, "What can *I* do?"
Dad said, "I want a second view."
GP replied, "You're ugly too."

If I could take life in my stride
As Dad; he just enjoys the ride
And still the whisky warms inside.

# THE STRANGER
## (Father at Seventy-Nine Years)

A woman phoned: "Two weeks it's been
Is he with you?"
No sign, not seen!
What can we do?

He must have died; just walked away . . .
Unwell and dropped.
We knew the day
Would come. He stopped . . .

. . . Us ever getting close. So date
With fate he kept.
For us? Too late
No hope, except!

The hospital; slim chance, but try.
"He's fine, he's well."
He did not die
We've gone through hell.

Our dad; he shrugs it off with ease
And should we say
"Be closer please"
He backs away.

# HOSPITAL VISIT
## (Whipps Cross, 18 February 1996)

We visited my father on this Sunday afternoon.
He seemed so lost and so was I
The pub did call; my mouth was dry
He looked all thin and weak "I must get out of here and soon."

We stayed; and he sat on the bed and found for us a chair.
It rather spoilt our routine day
For illness does get in the way
And then the conversation stopped and all we did was stare.

So lost for words we fidgeted and gazed around the ward.
Young nurses with bright eyes agleam
Dad's sense of humour reigns supreme
"I wonder how they cope with all this agèd flesh abroad."

The man is fit. At seventy-nine his zest for life is strong
This atmosphere of sickness seeps
The soul absorbs, the flesh it creeps
So he wants out before he's overwhelmed and swept along.

So may he leave? You've patched him up and thanks so very
much.
The thought would ever make him cringe
'Protruding vein; the dread syringe'
Admittedly a coward when it comes to jabs and such.

Now in a bar he is ensconced, almost as good as new!
So whisky warmed and spirits high
He phoned "I'll see you by and by."
And may you thrive for many years, old Dad, you rascal you.

# HERO IN A DIRTY MAC

He shuffled in from off the street
The rain drove hard; he smelt the eggs and beans.
Here's food that's fit for gods to eat!
"Just tea" (he'd lost the wherewithal and means).

Square meals were something of the past
One time a family and Sunday roast,
Clean sheets and things that wouldn't last.
Now come to this and giving up the ghost.

Who cares? When all is said and done
Who measures him? A god? He lost his soul!
He had one once, until he run
And found himself a dark deserted hole.

But true to his own self – a man
Who lived a lie then left a life behind.
A tear behind the mask, deadpan?
There's clownish laughter; deep-set eyes seem blind.

Now clearly he surveys the scene.
He sips his tea and contemplates the rain.
No thought of things that might have been?
Deep thinking maybe drives a brain insane!

'God's gold'; the whisky gets him through
A gulp en route to anywhere at all.
A pocket hero; faithful; true
"My screw-top saviour saves me when I fall."

There's truth in solitude and rain.
Affection is for fools and love was lost
Among the memories and pain.
All things of comfort he had then were tossed . . .

. . . Aside! He had no choice! How sweet . . .
The rain. And whisky gives a warmth that's real.
A handy bottle on the street
Far better to be numb than start to feel –

Square meals were something of the past
One time a family and Sunday roast,
Clean sheets and things that couldn't last.

# WARDEN-CONTROLLED

We thought we'd done what's best! He's getting old
We asked him would he like warden-controlled?
"Sheltered homes and wrinkled faces!" –
Now he hates the scene –
Claustrophobic airless places
Scrupulously clean!"

He seemed to like the idea at the start!
Community; a chance to be a part . . .
Short-lived! He says, "They're all brain-dead;
Chattering; inane.
I'd sooner read a book instead
Or I'd go insane.

"They never drink? I've never seen a cat!
No comfort there! I want no part of that!
I know I'm on the final lap
That don't bother me
There's more to life than endless yap;
Women drinking tea."

We made it nice; we did the best we could.
Explained it all, so Father understood:
"There's home helps and there's meals on wheels,
Should you have the need,
A cosy flat; no heating bills,
Luxury indeed!

"There's bingo and there's outings for the folk."
Our father is no ordinary bloke!
We've never known him to conform;
Slip into a slot.
Not him the norm! The uniform! . . .
Asking quite a lot . . .

. . . Expecting him to take it in his stride
We thought we'd done our best! We really tried!
He's grateful for the work we did;
Thanks us – in his way –
But no intention – God forbid –
Never will he stay.

We thought we did what's right! He's getting old
And soon he'll have no choice; **warden-controlled**!

## EPITAPH FOR MY FATHER, LESLIE CYRIL PEARCE
(23 March 1917 – 18 November 1998)

He had no faith, he cared not for his time;
He hungered for the moment, for the day.
He told me of the Church and of their crime:
"They hold their wealth while people slip away."
And now he's gone there's nothing left to say.

What's left? A prayer?
I wonder, did he pray?

# DAD'S FUNERAL

The vicar walked in front
His cassock flowing
Looked good beside
The undertaker man
They led the hearse
The wind was gently blowing
An end to my old dad's allotted span

He would have loved the sight
If he could see it
For centre stage
Is where he loved to be
Ironic, ashes scattered
So albeit
We moved away
To Bexhill on the Sea.

# VOID
(For My Father, Leslie Cyril Pearce)

There's just a void.
We used to have a drink.
I'm not annoyed!
We were never close,
We just were mates,
We had a drink.

There's just a void.
He had a soul, I think!
And yet he toyed,
In age he got morose,
But we were mates
And had a drink.

I'm not annoyed.
I miss him's what I think!
I'm not annoyed.
We were never close,
We just were mates,
We had a drink.

# EMPTY

She went so quick! Strange, staying in the flat:
Neglected; empty. Just days ago she was on the mend.
The phone – a final word "I'll see you soon." And that's the end?
We sorted through the clothes, the this and that.

We stayed among the clutter and the grime
The hollow rooms, reminders of the stark reality.
No more the smiling eyes, the pleasing hospitality.
Was someone ever here? Was there a time . . .

. . . When there was tea and food and warmth and Mum?
Nothing, gone, over, finished, done. What else is there to say?
She must have thought, 'My time has come, I'll quietly slip away.'
Describe the empty feeling? . . .

. . . Go for 'numb'!

# MATURITY

So now they're gone and now I come of age.
No matter they were troubled at the end
I'd sooner have them here – I'll not pretend.
Ol' Dad, he gave me laughs! Frustration! Rage!

And our dear mum, her life had turned a page –
Her problems all cleared up and on the mend.
Then, early morning, she left with a friend.
So *now* I'm grown? So *now* I come of age?

From 'always there' to 'gone for evermore'.
But life goes on – quick bursts of tears and grief.
The loss is mine; demand not an encore!
"We'll meet again" – how's that for bold belief?

There's no place in the plan to be alone
I have an instinct, more so now I'm grown.

# THE GHOSTS OF WINTER

I long for summer, even though I've yearned
For darker nights and warmth from firelight glow.
Now summer is a friend; my thoughts have turned
From winter – even though it's warmed me so.

My senses feel a chill unfelt before –
Short time ago we seemed such 'splendid hosts'
So suddenly comes death and grief and more
Come, summer, come! Dispel the winter ghosts.

Away for now! – This season's lost its charm –
Come, summer rain; come, sunlit days, and dwell.
Stay long enough, rejuvenate and calm
A haunted soul – too long in winter's spell.

They have more time to dwell when nights are long
Oh, soon come, summer, when the ghosts are gone.

# RAMPANT IN MY GENES

My thumping head . . . the night before
I had a brew or two
Or maybe it was three or four?
Well, surely quite a few.

Unwelcome you! You dreaded curse,
You drinkers' anti-friend,
Who makes the situation worse
And will not let me mend.

You poisoner of liver cells.
Destroyer of my brain.
Who takes my turbulence and quells
Then tempts: "Indulge again."

It's not my fault that I imbibe
That to the booze I leans (sic)
I'm offsprung from a drinking tribe
It's rampant in my genes . . .

. . . The scientists have made it clear
I never had a chance.
My mum and dad they like their beer
Much better than romance.

There's times when life can be real tough
Surviving day to day.
I'll be glad when I've had enough . . .
Lord, take the pain away.

# AUNTIE FLO AND UNCLE JOSH

We all lived in Blondin Street in Bow
When we were kids, so many years ago.
They must have been quite comfortable, they must have had
some dosh
Cos they had a car *and* telly; Auntie Flo and Uncle Josh.
We went on Sunday evenings; sat on cushions we would bring
And Dad would wear a gold milk top (he'd pawned his wedding
ring).
And Auntie Flo would stroke my ears whilst sat between her feet
And all of human life was there in dear old Blondin Street.

As kids we went, all those years ago.
We drove with Uncle Josh and Auntie Flo.
Wickford then was dusty lanes and summers seemed much hotter.
And Aunt and Uncle had some land and this shack called
'Charlotta'.
The grass was like a jungle and some farm girl had a horse.
She let me have a ride bareback; though young, I stayed the course.
The toilet was this Elsan thing; we used it till it filled.
Then Dad and Uncle dug a hole and dumped it in the field.

Mum and Dad and me and Sis would go
And this fat cat that Auntie named 'Bimbo'
And Uncle Josh had this small car with us all crammed inside.
Oh! what joy to leave the drab East End for gorgeous countryside.
We didn't care that running water never was on tap.
And 'Bimbo' seemed in perfect bliss asleep on Auntie's lap.
We'd spend our days adventuring and lie content at night
With pilchards and banana trifle gorged with great delight.

In her eighties now our Auntie Flo.
And Uncle Josh? He died long years ago.
Vague memories of a kindly man who always worked real hard.
Then they moved out to the country; open space; no cramped
backyard.
Now there's a modern bungalow and all this lovely land
With Auntie Flo and Uncle Harold – bless 'em – hand in hand.

I remember dusty lanes, when summers seemed much hotter. . . .
Holidays in Wickford in a shack they called 'Charlotta'.

# THREE BOYS

Georgie Kitchen, me and Kenny Stark
Just East End kids and our street was all right
But we were lucky we had Vicky Park.
Well! Vicky Park had us, but not at night.

And Vicky Park was welcoming and lush
Well, Vicky Park was much more than a friend,
All open, we were young and we would rush
And sad when dusk would bring it to its end.

We had a load of fun on summer days
Like queueing up to hire a rowing boat.
Skilled oarsmanship? Not quite, though we had ways
And looking back, did well to stay afloat . . .

. . . As, seamanlike, we set off round the lake
Disjointed, uncoordinated stroke.
Great gouged-up waves behind us in our wake
And even in the boat we got a soak.

Undaunted, we were lads, all fun and games.
At times there was a fairground after dark
The park and us three boys – remembered names –
Georgie Kitchen, me and Kenny Stark.

The lit-up rides, the dodgem cars would thrill
Loud rocking music, brightly flashing lights
Me, 'Jack the Lad', the man behind the wheel
And Vicky Park – exciting summer nights.

The rifle range: the weapon, loaded cork.
I'd seen the films, a cowboy I'd become.
I won a lot of statues made of chalk.
Great shiny dogs I took home to my mum.

Our park was all the countryside we knew
Enfolded us and wrapped us in its charm
A magic place, safe, watchful as we grew
Tall trees protective keeping us from harm.

All boys grow old yet our park doesn't age!
Though time just flew away as did we three
A memory from a photo-album page
Georgie Kitchen, Kenny Stark and me.

# BEATEN BEYOND RECOGNITION

I only ever saw him once; Bert Black.
He waved as we came through the door
He knew he'd seen her face before
Vague memory of someone he'd known way back?

A home for the bewildered and the lost.
He seemed quite fit at eighty-plus
Suspiciously he measured us
A brain in turmoil; life exacts a cost.

The others sat and stared; an old chap barked –
With sudden wit and clarity
As if it was normality –
"He thinks he is a dog," old Bert remarked.

"There's rabbits in the grounds, I see them run."
Was this some dream of younger days?
Of healthy youth and country ways?
Where now the lad? Now end had just begun.

And in the war he rode a motorbike
(We sat as he enjoyed his tea,
My wife asked Bert, "Do you know me?"
"Tomato soup with bread and jam I like."). . . .

He guided tanks at night did old Bert Black.
He little spoke of deeds of war.
But Belsen's hell we know he saw.
All simple now; and soon the heart attack.

We never got to see him any more.
He didn't know his daughter came
But pleased to see us all the same
He smiled and waved as we went out the door.

# MY 'SLIP' OF A WIFE

We have strolled in perfect peace down quiet country lanes
Just man and wife all warmed and quite content
Enjoying fragrant flowery scents enhanced by summer rains
And then she lost her grip and down she went.

And walking once through Goudhurst town she sauntered off alone
Just browsing as one does, then without warning,
My lovely wife, so careful as she treads on cobblestone,
Then bangs her head on some shop's low-slung awning.

She takes the tumbles in her stride! Though weakness there must be
She never would complain, nor never rankle
So elegant my lady, but yet it seems to me
To bring a whole new thought to 'turn of ankle'.

Right now she hobbles round the home, all swollen, pained and
bruised.
A shopping trip that ended in disaster.
We strode along and when she spoke these words I was amused,
"Please can we try to walk a little faster."

I fumbled; reached; to no avail, as down she went again.
Then lifted her and staggered to a seat.
I saw her little face turn white and longed to take her pain
This lovely lady cursed with two left feet.

Then ambulance to hospital; four hours we were there.
An X-ray and a check proved nothing broke.
Two crutches and a cloth support. "Just hop along, take care."
Excuse us if we just don't see the joke.

Her multicoloured ankle is not a pretty sight.
She makes no fuss and still walks with such grace.
Yet me, I'm ever nervous and hope next time I might
Just stop her falling flat upon her face.

# A FAMILY PORTRAIT

As statues, caught; life stilled and framed
Their faces masqued – all white; unnamed.
They all were living once, you know!
They all went with the ebb and flow;
All frozen now with ghostly stares
Our smiles shall be the same as theirs;
When, from an attic's dusty nooks,
Among the bric-a-brac and books
A photograph, a family group.
A posed, assembled little troop
Of nephew, uncle, aunt and niece,
Shall hang above a mantelpiece.

# LOLLIPOPS

They come on sticks, all shuffling, the old
All trembling hands
Where once the grasp was firm, no strength to hold.
What next? Bedpans!
And tubes stuck into veins and all the holes?

Cruel life. Who gave them strength! They didn't ask . . .
For splendid birth!
When, chubby-legged they tottered to their task
With infant mirth
Pathetic now, these sad and lonely souls.

Retirement; keen expectancy, they looked
Toward some ease
Tranquillity! Too much to ask. They're cooked!
No effort please.
No sporting now, not even gentle bowls.

Wheelchairs and pavement cars with batteries;
Stairlifts and baths . . .
With handles at the sides; all made to ease
Their wobbly paths.
What new directions now? What sought-for goals?

A wearing-down; a grinding to a halt
I bet there's more
I bet there's life renewed; the healthy sort
Beyond the door
I bet there's joy (at least the thought consoles).

Religion gives a hope, I s'pose it's real
I sometimes think,
'This isn't all.' Instinctively I feel
Some mystic link;
One act has gone! New stage; new set; new roles.

They shake on sticks; they smile; they feel the cold
And so shall we
The younger ones all waiting to grow old –
It tolls for thee –
The bell is struck! Ask not for whom it tolls.

# TIBBY

I never dreamed she'd ever go away.
A regal air; a cat at once serene.
A tortoiseshell; a beauty in her day.
At times aloof this splendid feline queen.

Bright morning and she warmed to early sun.
I could not watch her suffer any more.
Gone, childhood days and bright-eyed kitten fun.
I held her close; she softly placed her paw . . .

. . . Upon my breast and calmed my breaking heart.
Then silent in her basket; cease these tears!
She sensed that now had come the time to part.
And me? A whimpering child in adult years.

I left her on her own and she was scared.
And prayed, "God, let her know I really cared."

# REFLECTIONS ON PERFECTION

It's poetry and love within
that fills me full of cheer
My love, my deep affection
for a perfect pint of beer.

# CONTEMPLATING THE NAVEL

A dent, but yet a sexual glutton
Would delve into a belly button
The navel: such a simple thing
Not deep, perhaps worth pondering
Connected by a tube at birth
First neutral, then alive to earth
Erotic centre? That's enough!
It's just a hole that gathers fluff
Yet sultans long ago, I'm told,
Selected girls with skin of gold
With stomach ripe and navel deep –
They never did find time to sleep –
The belly dancer's wiggles would
Ensure that loins were stirred real good
It's different now, no mystery
The midriff's there for all to see
There's no holds barred with modern girls
Pierced bellies, artificial pearls
The nipple's also gone astray
It's seen in tabloids every day
When I was young I'd never come
Upon a daily baring bum
But times have changed and that's for sure
Young kids have seen it all and more
Too young, too soon, there's no excuse
We hold the guilt of child abuse
Enough for me to contemplate . . .
The navel, get a grip, old mate!

# THE COMFORT OF ANGELS

. . . And cupid kissed me
As I slept in sand
And dreamed of love
Cocooned in warmth
I'd drifted off
To somewhere far above

And I was heaven-bound
Where dreams are real
And angels care
For souls who've lost their way;
Who cannot cope
With life laid bare.

I'd left at last
Escaped from the said 'joys'
Of this good earth
No thing could draw me back
Just onward
To a sweet rebirth.

Then cupid kissed me
Such a sweet awakening
Such bliss
And all was new
And earth and heaven met
In one sweet kiss.

# AFD

I love my beer, I really do look forward to a glass.
My nerves are taut, my drinking fist is clenched.
Alcoholic constipation means: a pub I cannot pass!
But today's the day this thirst must stay unquenched.

My unease is apparent and my mind preoccupied
By Bacchus and his ilk I'm truly smote.
The urge keeps welling up in me. No matter how I've tried
I can't ignore this dryness in my throat.

So now and then I suffer; I put myself through hell!
"Be strong, you plonker, are you mouse or man?
This brief detoxication can only serve you well.
You have to do it, just to prove you can!"

To show I'm non-dependent is what it's all about.
That I still have the will to keep away.
"It's not too long! It goes real fast! Just watch me go without."
Thank God it's done! This 'Alcohol-Free Day'.

# PRIORITIES

If you should sit in Traffers Bar you'll know the sea is near;
You'll even have an inkling that the skies outside are clear;
An urge may grab you, now and then, to step outside and hear
The sound of seagulls shrieking! Let these thoughts not interfere
With all life's **real priorities** – we all know why we're here!?
To drink a glass, or two, or three before we disappear!
Good health to all in Traffers Bar; thank God for life and beer.

# THE RAT RACE FORGOTTEN

## MORNING:

In the garden; sunny bright
Flowering roses; creamy white
Dance their brilliance on the morning breeze
And so delight.

## AFTERNOON:

In the pub; cool pints of ale
Mild cigars; you don't inhale!
Good company and all is made to please
Let joy prevail.

## EVENING:

Back at home; will dinner bring
Sustenance fit for a king?
'Cooked to perfection' chicken, chips and peas
Does my heart sing?

## AND SO TO BED:

From the window; as I lay
White majestic roses sway –
Light-shadowed, soft, moon-kissed – to gently ease . . .
The day away.

# THE GOLDEN CURRY: THIS TREASURE TROVE OF WONDROUS SPICY FOOD

For many years we have warmed to your
Welcome and delighted in your excellence.
We have sought sustenance and we have relished
Your spicy wonders:

And we have tasted such delights
Ensconced in warmth and softened lights
Mouths watering for the joys to come
To gluttony we did succumb.

We piled our plates with meats and rice
And savoured dishes, flavoured spice.
Great mouthfuls relished, not in haste
Oh! One more taste, just one more taste.

Then slowly sipped a last liqueur
In comfort, as an epicure
And wishing for no more than this
Soft hours spent in utter bliss.

And when the taste buds start to yearn
To your delights may we return.

# LYNMOUTH TO COUNTISBURY (1996)

We trekked beside the river's rapid flow
Then took an upward route called Sparrow's Walk.
Steep; rising swiftly, seeing far below
The view; as from a predatory hawk.

Still climbing further, steeper, to the top
Among the quiet woodland, dense and deep.
Rejuvenated now, though fit to drop
We came across a lost and bleating sheep.

He turned and ran along the grassy edge
We trudged the muddy path quite close behind.
Then through the farmer's gate between the hedge
At last the welcome inn we sought to find.

The journey's end; a ploughman's and a tear
Exorbitant the price and bad the beer.

## SONNET TO WETHERSPOON
(From an appreciative CAMRA member)

I've led a drinker's life; I have a view
Unbiased; I discern a decent drop.
I sup a glass or two of savoured brew.
Not alcopop! Nor fizzy lager top!
But crafted ales of barley, malt and hop
Real living brews; traditional and good.
Guest beers like 'Brewer's Droop' and 'Belly Flop'.
Imbibers? We are oft misunderstood.
Our pleasure we take seriously and would
Search out the friendly taverns day or night
And joyfully befriend a brotherhood.
Piped background noise would put us all to flight.
So tempt us with your quality and flair.
J. D. . . . it's very comforting you're there.

# ALL DEAD (1997)

Dave's beard was black and Guinness was his brew;
Old Neville drank whatever was at hand.
He ran a pub and Fridays, with the band,
He'd play the trumpet – sing a song or two.

And Keith drank Burton – more than just a few.
So slim the lad – his legs could hardly stand.
A barman with a smile; a willing hand.
He died so young, I can't believe it's true!

Such nice men; heavy drinkers – bless 'em all.
All gone now; shuffled off this mortal coil.
Far better gone than time and age could spoil!
An exit quick; no slow decline and fall.

Look down, you lads! Look down! Remember me?
I grew that beard and live beside the sea.

# WINTER WARMER
(A Sonnet)

Come soon, bleak winter, let me feel your bite
I will not curse the dark nights nor the chill.
My cup is offered, with your treasures fill
That I may sup the goodness then delight.

Large-measured whiskies; glowing firelight
Rich golden ales brewed strong – with joy instil
Embrace me with your warmth and all goodwill
Then I shall glow with comfort Christmas night.

Wrapped warm; I see the beauty of your days
The magic wand that's waved by nature's hand
Again a child and wide-eyed still I gaze
Crisp frosted mornings; winter wonderland.

Bright-starred your mystic nights – the heavens shine
On moonlit snow and all is peace divine.

# ILLUMINATION

A sheltered haven's beacon bright
Where calmness quells the soul's dark night.

# DEAD POETS

We living poets do our best
Incentive there is not
Financial gain? Hold, sir, you jest!
Reward? There's not a lot!

Dead poets have it all *their* way
They made their mark then left
Now plagiarists cannot dismay
In death there is no theft.

Sweet death; sweet dreams; sweet comatose
Sweet, lost in space and time
Sweet verse; sweet lifting up from prose
Sweet poems – with a rhyme.

Dead poets all had charm enough
Oh could I write like Keats
Enough's enough I've written stuff
But now there's nought but cheats.

I pray you'll resurrect the verse
Bring beauty to our time
Forget us not. For bad or worse
We're lost without a rhyme.

# OLD MAN IN PUB: STILL LIFE

Complains, "It's cold."
Losing it, lived too long
Complains, "The music's loud."
Pathetic, old
Complaining, "It's all wrong."
Still . . . comfort in a crowd.

Mostly alone
At home. Death closing in.
He says he's "seen the man" –
But still he's prone
To fantasy and gin –
He says he's "glimpsed the plan".

He's summer-dressed
A buttonhole as well
Looks quite a dapper chap.
He needs a vest
And warmth. But, what the hell
His brain's in overlap.

Still sharp; aware
"I'm ninety-five" he's proud
He hopes to slip away
Not quite sure where –
Where pubs are not so loud
And tranquil is the day.

## SUSPICION OF TRUTH

If God forgives everybody and every sin, then perhaps my natural instincts lead me to the Devil! At least, hopefully, he will let the evil bastards burn in hell.


You tell me a Man lived who knew only love!
Resisted all temptation!
Who sought the word of God from heaven above
In quiet contemplation!

I tell you, if such a Man lived,
He must have been a God!

# AWAKENING
### (Blest Are They Who Have Not Seen, yet Believed)

And God could hold me if He would
And He could take me far away
And settle me in softness
As a child; and wonder as I play.

Yet He will leave me floundering!
And does He gloat and take delight?
Sadistically enjoying
Seeing children frightened of the night.

Yet night-time slowly turns to day
So infant fear will surely fade
As eyes become accustomed
And the darkness holds the voice that prayed.

And God will hold me when He can
And He will take me far away
And bless me as I wonder
As the magic light reveals the day.

# ALL IS FORGIVEN?

Are we special? We the destroyers
Why should we be saved?
What right have we to pray
Forgive? And all our sins be waived.

We are special!! We! The employers,
Users of the earth
Who take it all and waste
And kill. Treat all with little worth?

Then did a godly Man appear
And walk among us without fear
And did He have a sacred way
A calmness? Though He could not stay
Yet did He love us nonetheless?
Though we destroyed, still, He did bless.

# THE KISS OF FAITH

Death:
Have I known you from the start?
Aware of your faint steady beat!
Relentless; you shall cease the heart
Attach your tag on yellowed feet.

Death:
Have you made your presence known?
When shocked awake and all is stilled.
And was the seed so early sown?
That straight from birth all life is killed.

Death:
Haunting in a ghostly shroud
Who whispers in the dead of night
"Waste not your time on prayers – head bowed,
'Tis I who will shut out the light."

Faith:
Have I known you from the start,
Aware of your faint steady beat
Pulsating stronger to impart
That maybe you will death defeat?

Faith:
Have you made your presence known?
When dread is all and fear abounds
And has your gentle comfort grown?
To overwhelm – dark whispered sounds.

Faith:
Hovering ever watchful now
Safe-keeping in the dark of night,
"Forsaken not, I promise thou,
'Tis I will lead you to the light."

# TRINITY

## SCIENCE

Too much for ordinary souls?
Equations algebraic
Explaining things about the speed of light.
No interest in great black holes
Nor spectrumed light, mosaic
Viewed bright through telescopes in darkest night.

Enough that there are power brains
Who delve beyond the layers.
Such physicists who boggle humble minds.
These special ones whom God ordains
Phenomenal star-players.
Prof. Hawking, sir, the science ever blinds!

And grab this logic if you can
Then comprehend the meaning.
A young boy pondered on a dream, until
(A genius this Einstein man)
Through theoretic gleaning,
Proved; at the speed of light all time stands still.

# GOD

But God – who knows all space and time
And worlds beyond dimension,
Who spake the word, then laid out all the rules;
Delivered us through heat and slime;
Inanimate suspension –
Surveys us as a motley bunch of fools!

God watches us. And evidence
Proves what a sense of humour!
Creating monster man endowed with lust.
This throbbing mass of decadence;
One vast malignant tumour.
Will all become explained when we are dust?

Shall we *all* know of mighty things?
Of infinite Creation?
As, spirit-like, we traverse astral spheres.
Enlightened, as our Maker brings
Such vivid explanation
Of – what it all was for – the earthly years.

# THE MEANING OF LIFE

. . . So did I love my fellow man;
Avoid discrimination?
And was I tolerant of different ways?
I strove to see the perfect plan
Of nation helping nation.
And *may* have done some good things in my days!

It matters not. . . . The earth evolves
Progressively regressive.
Scientists are ever delving deeper.
But simple basic truth involves
All actions non-aggressive;
Everyone should be his brother's keeper.

And what of love? This mystic thing
Beyond the dread equation!
God gave us life; a chance for Him to teach;
To sow a seed; that fruit may spring
Just gently, with persuasion;
Perfection – is the aim beyond our reach?

# SOUL-SEARCHING

Where lies this everlasting thing, my soul?
(Whom flesh releases, come my silent heart
Then flies to God who makes my spirit whole)
Where are you hidden; in what vital part?

What camouflage this sacred thing must wear!
Disguised so well! For I have searched within
In contemplation deep and lost in prayer
I looked in vain and found just mortal sin.

You guarded well your purity, you laid
Such decoys – or was this the Devil's plan
That in my vanity I saw displayed
A saintly symbol; not a lowly man?

Oh! Come the great unveiling shall I see
The mystery, the beauty that is me?

# THE BOSS

Such thunder rolled across the blackened sky
The devils danced and sensed the night was theirs.
No hint! They had no corner to their eye!
An angel stepped on bright celestial stairs . . .

Just out of sight. These demons took no heed
And whilst they played their games, with ill intent,
God's light illumined all their evil deed.
Then spake this purest soul, "You must repent,

"And cease your diabolic doings now!
Before it is too late! Leave nought to chance!"
The devils heard at last, then took a bow
But heeded not; just carried on their dance.

And though they frolicked, joy would be their loss
God took a note! . . . And God knows who is Boss!

# FAITH AS AGAINST PROOF

God bless you all, you seekers of the truth,
For you belong to God as does the world
Delve deep and search for paranormal proof
And pray you'll see the mystery unfurled.

Check out the OBEs and NDEs
Experiment in depth with ESP
And leave no stone unturned, I beg you, please,
For we who seek the truth can't wait to see . . .

. . . Results from all your delvings. Have you found
Some pattern that would prove that there is psi?
Some disembodied ultrasonic sound;
We may be here and if we are, please, why?

A ghost appears! Yet surely just a dream?
Imagination plays such naughty tricks
Was that a tortured soul? I heard a scream!
The other world is playing pick and mix.

Set up the probes though be aware of fraud
Sophisticated charlatans will try
All devious means to spread their word abroad
That souls of loved ones dwell beyond the sky.

And skies contain a mystery so deep
That clouds can form a shadow like a wraith.
So are we saved, or just eternal sleep?
The proof is never proved, there's only faith.

# KINGS AND CLOUDS

I never understood the shapeless things.
Then saw Adonis rise, but as a cloud;
From over roofs, and close behind a crowd
And all of them had wondrous angels' wings
And what a joy a heaven's vision brings.
Still, there were times such darkness, like a shroud
I never understood!

I never understood the rumblings . . .
Of skies, until I looked more deep and ploughed . . .
The heavens with my eager eye. Then loud . . .
Would boom the voice of all! The King of Kings!

I never understood.

# THE SWEET SCENT OF LOVE

I know You not, You Christ! I cannot walk
With You as with a friend and softly talk,
For You are gone. Yet You are here! But where?
I cannot touch and even though I stare
I shall not see, for You are far above.
Still . . . do I catch the scent of Your sweet love
And do You guide me as the silent Friend,
And love me even to the very end?

# COME; THY KINGDOM

Can anyone make sense at all of living for life's sake?
And can there be a reason for one's birth?
Such comfort in the womb and then so rudely slapped awake
You're welcomed to the world for what it's worth.

Apparently we are lost souls – just waiting for a turn
To make amends another time around –
Who cocked it up in lives gone past, so still there's more to learn!
And if we pass *this* test we're heaven-bound. . . .

This heaven thing sounds good to me
No work; unburdened; floating free!
Oh, please, dear Lord, don't let me be
Forever trapped in purgatory.

Reserve a place for those of us
Alighting from life's omnibus
Who bore the brunt with little fuss
And didn't moan and didn't cuss.

For even as each day begun
(A constant search for selfish fun
Head hung with shame; the Devil won)
I always prayed, "Thy will be done."

And prayed not as an afterthought
But prayed, believing prayers are caught,
And self-control is not for nought,
And saintliness cannot be bought.


I've surely been here many times yet still I am impure
Though almost perfect! Almost like a saint!
It's lust, and sloth, and food, and beer that holds me back, I'm sure
Okay, okay! A saint is what I ain't.


So, Lord; who sees our every move; the smooth stuff and the rough.
Who picks us for eternity sublime
Shall You yet say, "You did quite well but not quite good enough
So try again, My son, just one more time"?

# A MIGHTY MAN

From His vantage point on high
A Mighty Man looked down
Great tears welled from His caring eye
"Creation moves My heart to cry . . .
There's heaven for you when you die . . .
You've heard of My renown!"

There were some that He could see
Who wore the holy cloth;
Who bowed their head and bent their knee
Whilst offering a fervent plea
Who gave 'with all sincerity'
But falsely pledged their troth!

He would prompt and He would nudge
He'd show a guiding light.
The evil ones He couldn't budge;
Too steeped in decadence and sludge
They sneered that He could be their Judge
And tears would smear His sight.

"Hey, listen up, I dare you!"
He boomed across the land.
"I own a place where skies are blue
Believe Me all My words are true
I have a place to offer you
Come, trust Me, take My hand."

From his view below the earth
An evil one looked up
And cursed all for their lowly birth
Implied their lives had little worth
Then chuckled with real nasty mirth,
"Here, take my potent cup."

Tempted with forbidden fruit;
Enslaved by greed and lust.
Sad volunteers he would recruit;
A ragged band of ill repute
And from his mouth such lies would shoot,
"You must trust me! You must!"

He would rant and he would rave,
"There is no promised land!
There's no one for your soul to save!"
He'd try it all, this scurvy knave,
But some were strong and some were brave
And took a mighty stand.

Armed with faith and valour great
To battle they did go.
They pledged to fight, with love not hate
To compromise then infiltrate
No evil would they contemplate
To beat the dreaded foe.

Yet, defeated after all
Kind thoughts could not compete
For demons would entice, enthral
So all the world could have a ball
Unheeding of our Saviour's call
"Your joy is bittersweet!"

Once upon a special time
A Mighty Man looked down
All love and hate had reached a prime
To carry on would be a crime
All life is Mine; all love sublime
"You've heard of My renown."

# FRONT-LINE PRAYER

Our Father who art in heaven, what gives?
"Keep up and hold the line, we are as one!"
Our Father who art in heaven, who lives?
'Tis not the man who knows his foe nor gun
For sure as eggs are eggs he will be done . . .
(And nought but fate will lift the soldier high) . . .
Be done before the battle has begun!
Though stepping bravely, gloriously die.
Thy kingdom come and swift their souls should fly
Gone, God knows where, but hallowed be *their* name
There's no more sacred ground than where they lie
And warrior or saint! What's in a name?
Shall trespass be forgiven at the end?
Where no-man's-land is welcome to a friend?

# GALLIPOLI
## (The Nek, 7 August 1915)

The whistle blew, they scrambled up, then instantly fell back.
They took the deadly armament full force.
The desert sand a deathbed for the powerless Anzac.
Though gallant was the regiment (Light Horse).

He'd stood in line and waited, braced, then swallowed back his fear
This time was his, he'd jump aloft and run.
He grasped a kind of meaning, yet his mind was still unclear
He raced till he was shattered by the gun.

Brave lives are ever wasted by atrocities of war.
And volunteers know not of things from hell.
Of fire-breathing monsters; nor the giant dragon's roar,
And loyalty would never serve them well.

All dead! The running soldiers; the young men come to fight.
All gone to waste! How futile the attack!
And bloodied red the desert sand, transformed from virgin white
And gallant were the powerless Anzac.

# REMEMBERING THE INNOCENTS OF DUNBLANE
## (13 March 1996)

"It doesn't seem right – they were only in school
Little kids learning
Then all shot to death – teacher and all
Gone! . . . Never returning."

We grieve and cry
Yet those who die
Have left behind the pain.

For peace is theirs
All worldly cares
Are gone. . . . They live again.

Through faith we too shall find peace.

# LOVE

And age will just enhance the pleasure which is ours
Pray, may we dwell awhile? The wonder ever flowers.
*'This Love Did Find Us'*

# HOLD TIGHT TO LOVE,
# FOR LOVE MAY SLIP AWAY

Hold tight to love, for love may slip away
(Though thoughts may trouble you and say love's gone)
Keep close to warmth for coldness will dismay
In loneliness there's time to dwell upon . . .
The loving looks and magic stars that shone
The dream that's lost can devastate your mind
Hold very tight lest love and warmth be gone.

There was real love; a quiet, softer kind
And warmth was never very far behind
Hold close for soon enough all love has dried
And lovers who have lost are groping, blind
Whoever said that love was smooth had lied
There's stumbling blocks and paths that seem unclear
Hold tight to love, for love can disappear.

# AND GOD CREATED WOMAN . . .

. . . Who may calm me with a look
Then comfort with a touch.
Guilt is mine that I have took
For granted far too much.

No gallant knight with armour
Bright; no heart-throb actor.
Yet my love sees a charmer,
Warms to feel-good factor.

She has eyes that look with care
Upon my wretched face.
Bemoans not my lack of hair.
Yet with an angel's grace . . .

. . . Adores me. I am raised high.
I am lifted above
And intoxicated by
Her emanating love.

# YOUNG LOVE: CLOSE ENCOUNTERS OF THE FIRST KIND

She was there when I was young
And she did tempt this callow youth.
Her skin was fair, her beauty sung
Of simple innocence and truth.

This slender girl with Irish eyes
I watched in secret, all was new.
My brain did whirl with pained surprise
And trembling knew not what to do.

Then soon to hold such tiny hands
And smell her female fragrance near
Still yet more bold we walked the sands
Exquisite joy replaced the fear.

And did I taint this special one?
When I was hers and bliss was mine.
And was faint innocence undone?
Whilst in the park at summertime.

As warmed and thrilled we would embrace
All new; to touch and closely lie
And all was stilled in time and space
Though we reclined our souls would fly.

So thus we bonded for a while.
We 'owned' each other 'wondrous years'
Till love absconded – ran a mile
A shattered dream and bitter tears

Passed long ago, just memory
My mind still wanders deep among
The hazy glow of reverie
When she was there and I was young.

# CONCERNED WITH LOVE

Long past; the novelty of innocence
And all the bittersweet-ness of our youth
Naivety replaced by inner sense
Now time enough to learn of love and truth.

For truth and love are blended soon; and stay.
Not fragile joined; to break at any whim
Not rent asunder by some darkened day
But strengthened more as brightness starts to dim.

Too soon in younger years is love thought caught.
Too soon are pledges made that may not hold
When promised oaths and fragile truths are fraught
With signs that passioned warmth will run to cold.

But now that we are done with childish stuff
To learn of love and truth; there's time enough.

# SONNET FOR MY LOVE

Could I express my thoughts with words that rhyme?
Would I do justice to what's dear to me?
Grant me forever! Or a longer time!
Still would I strive to send my heart to thee.

Though we are here we shall not ever be.
Though life is richer each and every day.
But maybe love is like eternity
And good things never ever fly away.

Our God is good, He listens when we pray.
He bends His ear for truth He does perceive.
Take 'cherish', such an easy word to say
Then 'love' and 'worship' – all that I believe

Oh, could I move your soul with stirring stuff!
I write the words, but words are not enough.

# WHAT LOVE?

What love have I if You are gone? What love
Could lift me high; lay soft against my rage?
What soul would comfort me? What soul above
Lies waiting, and from heav'n would disengage
Swoop down and hold me in my hour of need?

No love could hold me if You went! No soul
Would care enough to lend an ear and heed
The wailing of a heart no longer whole!

And I would be alone; and I would grieve . . .
Too long. For shattered hearts may never mend
Till angels with their ways shall make believe
That all is well and love will never end.

What life have I if You are gone; what will?
Save You are there, and faith brings comfort still.

# THE JOURNEY BEGINS

He wakened – kind of misty – then he caught
A glimpse, just fleeting at first.
'Can't be! I must still be dreaming,' he thought.
But then reality burst
Upon him. She seemed more beautiful now –
He had not seen her for years –
Rejuvenated! Full of life! But how?
Beguiled, he was moved to tears.

She knew he would come to find her at last.
She waited. They had loved deep
And grown together in times long, long past.
She'd left, but would always keep
Watching; waiting. Now she could show him things.
She'd seen him awake confused
With the fear disorientation brings
And his body old; misused.

Now was the beginning. He would grow young
And they would walk through such sweet
Blossom-scented summer lanes; dwell among
The glorious and complete
Beauty of it all. No grieved sad goodbye
Would again shatter the heart.
Their lives were lived and then, the time to die
And now the living would start.

# ON READING KEATS'
# 'THE TERROR OF DEATH'

Your thoughts on love and fame and death confound
You never lived to taste the fruits of life:
To see your 'Poems on the Underground'
To take your dear beloved as a wife. . . .

That I could be as clever with my pen
Reflecting on a cloudy shadowed moon
Alas! Your skills escape me, so I yen
Refreshment in a J. D. Wetherspoon.

Yet I have been more fortunate in love
Though fame eludes me there is sweet solace
I've traced romantic symbols from above
And chanced upon such lovingness and grace.

And I shall need her ere I may draw breath
And keep her love beyond the veil of death.

# POTPOURRI

And on it goes, this constant strain,
this striving to be noted.
To join the great poetic train:
gold-plated; silver-coated . . .

*'Dilemma'*

# THE CONQUEROR BUTTERFLY

He's black and white and dangerous (though this is quite absurd)
A 'hunter' he lies still upon the ground
He creeps among the undergrowth, low, stalking for a bird
Real watchful; making not a move nor sound . . .
A flutter caught his eye; he spun around.

A wafted leaf, moved by the breeze, had settled near a log
'But surely leaves don't hop about, and croak!'
So, Felix pounced! And tooth and paw revealed a humble frog.

This pussycat! A killer? What a joke!
And then it rained, so Felix got a soak!

Next day the garden beckoned – though he had a cold and cough –
The hunter watched the flutterings on high.
He thought he'd try his paw again (the frog had taken off)
And birds would fly too high and flutter by
But Felix *could* claw down a butterfly.

This tiny thing with milky wings and fragile body parts
Was no match for a scoundrel such as he.
He liked to toy and torment, did this naughty knave of hearts
Though cats are killed by curiosity!
Just then, he turned to scratch away a flea.

This butterfly had magic, so she waved her fairy wand
And instantly a pussy willow tree . . .
Appeared. No sign of Felix! Did this artful cat abscond?
Or was he planted, ever more to be
A home for all the bird fraternity?

It stands there in the garden as the seasons come and go
And all our little feathered friends enjoy . . .
The pussy tree. They sit and sway on branches to and fro
Remembering when they could well annoy . . .
Young Felix. . . . He was such a naughty boy!

# RACHEL'S APPLE PIE

I've been transported to another realm
A pastry case that's succulently full . . .
Of apple chunks. The taste would overwhelm . . .
An epicure, would even make him drool.

And as for me? I'll slice one splendid wedge
Eat heartily, lip-smacking fruit and crumb
Devouring all till nothing's left I pledge
Another portion? Who could not succumb?

Such humble food, a simple apple pie
A certain touch has turned it to a dream
With custard sauce in splendour it may lie
Or really naughty – topped with clotted cream.

Home cooking: in my heart a special place
You certainly can fill a pastry case.

# PUBLISH AND BE DAMNED

I wrote a book of verse a while ago
A crafted work – it seemed to take an age.
Reflecting back – 'You stupid so and so,
'Twas doggerel you put upon the page!'

Some foolish dream of taking centre stage,
An ego trip! Of mortal man a curse!
Such vanity, whatever could assuage
The driving force? Things went from bad to worse.

A book evolved called *Making Matters Verse*
One copy sold, or maybe even two!
No jackpot here; no great prizewinning purse,
But still, I made the ninety-nine *Who's Who?*

The door's still slightly open, not quite slammed
Strong impulses poetic . . . I'll be damned!

# TELEPHONE: SUNDAY AFTERNOON
(Spain to Bexhill-on-Sea, 4 February)

Ralph is dying
We're both crying
News from sunny Spain
We've just had beers –
So quick come tears –
We walked home in the rain

And then the call –
Some hope but small –
How fast you sober up –
The cancer's hit
Oh, bloody shit!
What else to do but sup?

We're caught off guard
It's quick and hard
A bolt from out the blue
So fit and well
So, what the hell!
It's only death, that's true.

# IT'S ALL GREEK TO ME (2002)

Les, this poem is translated from my Greek book.

On the secret seashore
White like a pigeon
We thirsted at noon
But the water was brackish.

On the golden sand
We wrote her name
But the sea breeze blew
And the writing vanished.

With what spirit, what heart
What desire and passion
We lived our life: a mistake!
So we changed our life.

Ernie, not translated from the Greek.

On the Bexhill seafront
Covered in seagull s--t (droppings)
We were dying for a pint of Harveys
And the sea was crashing

The pebbled beach
Rejected all attempts
At writing names
In the sand

So we changed our approach
We channelled our desire
And slaked our thirst
For passion . . .
A pint in Traffers.

# METAMORPHOSIS

Clean-cut I was a while ago, employed as a cashier;
White-collared, I 'belonged' to Hackney Borough.
I grit my teeth and got stuck in for nearly twenty year.
I looked the part; the brainwashing was thorough.

I tried to don the happy mask and mostly did succeed.
The customers would queue to see my face
And droves of people, when I left, did bow and scrape and plead –
"The likes of you they never could replace!"

But I knew well another door was opening for me,
And though it was 'real tough' to break away . . .
The call had come – hang up your stamp and write great poetry –
No choice had I but humbly to obey.

Now, I have written brilliant verse, I've mastered rhyme and scan,
And sonnets that would move the hardest heart.
Yet now they say, "You've got it wrong, it's all old-fashioned, man."
The modernists would tear my work apart!

But this boy's not for budging, though it drives me to despair.
John Betjeman decried the 'with-its' prose –
And likewise I will soldier on, for blank verse I don't care!
TRADITIONALISTS KNOW JUST HOW TO COMPOSE.

And if my friends could see me now, the transformation's weird!
No more the clean-cut look of long ago
But Moses-like; a cultivated growth of flowing beard
And hair that never had a chance to grow!

'Twas never meant that I should be ambitious in my job
Collecting rent's not what life's all about.
From just the slightest murmur to a great pulsating throb!
This 'poet', from inside, came bursting out!

# A CURLY CAT

I have a curly cat, he's made of stone.
A friendly chap of gentle tooth and paw.
He sleeps beside the door all on his own.
He asks for peace and quiet, nothing more.

He'll tolerate a touch but not too much!
He'd rather stay unnoticed if he may.
And little furry things like mice and such
Would please him if they'd only go away.

# DESPAIR

I sense a faint affinity
My instincts tell me so
I snuggle down with books between the sheets

What blasphemy! A trinity:
There's Edgar Allan Poe,
And me, Les Pearce, and good old Cockney Keats

A threesome of poetic worth!
I bow my head in shame
And ask forgiveness ever to have thought . . .

. . . That I! A one of lowly birth
Could ever be a flame
And light a soul; nay, I fall rather short . . .

. . . Of expertise, of genius;
I never could compete
With wordsmiths who could shape the magic phrase

I'd face the world abstemious!
To savour skills as sweet
That I could hold such honour in my days!

I'd have it now whilst I am here
And not when life is gone
I'd wallow in the glory and the fame

And when at last I disappear
There'd be no signed 'Anon'
He lived; he wrote; and Les Pearce was his name.

# MAKING MATTERS VERSE

The very stuff of my brain is rhyme
I 'think' in verse
Fearful of age and time
With the curse . . .

. . . Of memory lapses;
Frustration; grasping at straws
Confidence collapses
Brain cells cede to natural laws.

But yet the prize does lie within
Though deeper hid
And still to delve therein
Lost amid . . .

. . . The murk of stagnant thought.
To seek the glimmering light
Still further have I sought
The star that twinkles in the night

Oh! For the gift of clearer sight.

# SONNET

If only I could be a sonneteer!
All rhythmic; a beginning and an end
Not deep and cryptic like the modern trend
Old-fashioned rhyme; traditional and clear
Or even if I could get somewhere near!
Some just reward for hours that I spend
Please, Mr Shakespeare, would you be my friend
And whisper your trade secrets in my ear?

Syllabic content; ten to every line
Just fourteen lines; no major epic task
Yet disciplined and flowing smooth and fine
To be a sonneteer is all I ask.

Stopped short! The poem ends, the 'bard' resigns
Unless, of course, we're counting these two lines.

# SONNET TO 'JANUS'

I've been accused of moving goalposts; true.
So now it's coming real, a foolish dream
   An acorn planted; cultivated, grew.
   Not yet an oak, but modestly supreme,
And dare I mention smug-faced cats and cream?
From whence did inspiration flow? . . . Don't ask.
But through the tunnel did I spy a gleam?
And looking back it seemed a hopeless task.
Then Janus with his double-headed masque . . .
Bade: "Enter and together we will strive."
(Just one small taste of fame! Just one brief bask!)
"We'll do our best to keep your hope alive."

And soon the dream I thought I'd never see
MY book of verse . . . MY published poetry.

# SONNET FOR MY DENTIST

She digs and delves; she drills and scrapes away.
She plugs and fills and crowns the whole day through
To keep the dreaded tooth decay at bay
And make neglected molars look like new.

Great gaping mouths with pyorrhoea gums;
This battlefield of wounded, sick and dead
So skilfully the lady overcomes
She ventures forth where brave men fear to tread.

White-faced I've sat within the waiting room
And cringed to hear the screaming of the drill.
Then pondered on my own forthcoming doom,
Regretting having never made a will.

Brave! . . . I face this orthodontic venture.
Save the tooth; frustrate the dreaded denture.

# WALTHAMSTOW WALK

He found the quiet places, off the beaten track;
He walked the towpath by the water's edge;
He trudged the muddy footpaths discovered round the back,
And left behind the neat trimmed privet hedge.

The winter mornings braced him; his pace was firm and strong.
Invigorated now his body glowed.
His breathing, hard though steady, propelled him swift along
Deserted walkways hidden from the road.

He'd grown a little idle; enjoyed the lazy life . . .
Of late, a stab of pain around his chest . . .
Inspired him to exercise; stay healthy for the wife
And put his creaking body to the test.

He'd wait till all was quiet. The kids in their schoolrooms,
And all the workers safely in their place.
He'd slip around the side streets to avoid the traffic fumes
Then ponder on this sad old human race!

He always thought too deeply of God and love and death.
A friendly soul who never could unwind.
A nervous individual since ever he drew breath
Dark-shadowed were the pathways of his mind.

He wondered where he came from and what it all was for
And would there be a meaning at the end?
The way ahead confused him, he'd not been here before!
He couldn't see the path beyond the bend.

"No turning back, press onward," the voice within him urged.
So on he walked discovering new ground.
The open marsh, Lea Valley, in front of him emerged
And here was peace, with not a human sound.

So solitude's the answer? (Monastic was his thought)
A hermit-like existence – all remote;
To brave the harshest weather, of comfort caring nought
And then it rained, and him without a coat!

He sensed that he was destined to take an awkward route.
Instinctively he knew that he might stray.
But he was no crusader; no iron-willed Canute.
So bravery must wait another day.

He pushed across the marshland, then broke into a trot
Then on towards Chalk Bridge, still jogging fast.
His legs were getting heavy and his skin was sticky hot.
No sign of pain! His heart was made to last.

"I've watched him in his travels; I've been inside his mind;
I've kept the profile low for his own sake.
I've been real close, but always stayed a step or two behind
Intrigued to see the road that he would take.

"He doesn't know he's followed, yet he leans towards belief.
He fears the Father, Son and Holy Ghost.
Now homeward-bound; a haven from the thoughts that cause
him grief
His wife; strong tea and thick hot buttered toast."

# A MOVING SONNET

Dream on about the coast and living there
Where London's fumes and grime shall never taint.
Escape and dwell and breathe such pleasant air
Where poets are inspired and painters paint.
Where time seems slower-paced and all is quaint.
"Hark, dream no more, for I have heard your plea" –
So spake the fervent dreamer's patron saint –
"I have a place called Bexhill on the Sea,
And herein lies your dreamed tranquillity."

So move, you urban dweller; wrench away
And salvage basic things; like sanity.
Then breathe again and live another day.

Dislodge me from this rut, this life-etched groove
Uproot my stubborn soul; to seaward move.

# POETIC IMPULSE

I seem to spend a lot of time
Withdrawn and deep in thought.
Soul-searching for the perfect rhyme
The deeply moving sort.

No choice have I, I am compelled
To seek the special phrase.
I'm driven by some force, impelled
The search can last for days . . .

. . . Or weeks, or months, who knows how long?
It steers a natural course
And almost carries one along
By disembodied force.

And therein maybe lies the clue
Perhaps the hand does write
Thus animated – 'strange but true?' –
By mystic inner sight.

So true poetic impulse drives
And prompts the soul 'transcend',
Enrich, enliven humble lives
And thus: the verse must end.

# DIANA RECLOTHED

She held the fevered child; she felt despair.
She touched the sick; this magical princess.
She searched her soul – God, let them see I care!
So fair of face, she wore a golden dress.

"Divest me of my robe; this priceless gown!
That all the poor may benefit from wealth.
I seek no glory nor a queenly crown
Save; feed the hungry; grant the sick ones health . . .

". . . Then clothe me not in satin, silk or lace
But with your spirit guide my caring hand
Endow me with such lovingness and grace
Embolden me with strength that I may stand . . .

". . . In raiment plain; enshrouded as a nun
Then, I behold! My journey has begun."

# THE POET'S DREAM

I offer no apologies
Ambition drives me on
I've 'graced' a few anthologies
And ever seized upon
The chance to drive my message home
To put my thought across;
Immortalised in textured tome
Where golden words emboss
And shine upon the parchment page;
Such beauty in the flow
Coordinated lines engage;
Enthral the reader so!

I dreamed I had a magic pen
And wrote a magic word.
Then wakened in a world of men
Where dreams become absurd.

# NOT A-MUSING

"Is the muse upon you?"
I was asked, "Where is the muse?"

It's gone, without a clue
What's upon me is the booze!

# FACELESS (2006)

The pain and the passion:
You'll catch it if you look close enough beyond the façade
Eyes: the windows to the soul. Look deep. . . .
Life, after a fashion:
You'll maybe catch a glimpse of a slum kid in a backyard
Something creeps into us as we sleep.

Changes come fast through years.
There is no comparison to the person I was then . . .
And am right now! Whatever occurred?
Time! Age! Love! Laughter! Tears!
All poured into life; overfilled. I forgot to say when . . .
And in the beginning was the word.

Now I'm taken over:
A different face; a different me. Who am I meant to be?
What happens at the end of the play?
One lost soul? A rover?
One tiny craft in the great vastness of the open sea?
Faceless, without form? No night nor day. . . .

Where do I go from here?
There's an idea that heaven is all I need (so lonely)
Can I be certain of such a thing?
(Lots of rumours you hear.)
God's love: a lifeline for the soul. Friends, angels (if only).
Perhaps nothing! Death, here is thy sting.